TRAINING WITH TREATS

Transform Your Communication,
Trust and Relationship

Published in the United States by 14 Hands Press,

an imprint of Camp Horse Camp, LLC

www.14handspress.com
Some of the material herein has appeared
in other books by Joe Camp

Library of Congress subject headings

Camp, Joe

Training with Treats by Joe Camp

Horses

Human-animal relationships

Horses training

Horsemanship

The Soul of a Horse: Life Lessons from the Herd

ISBN 978-1-930681-44-6

First Edition

TRAINING WITH TREATS

*Transform Your Communication,
Trust and Relationship*

JOE CAMP

14 HANDS PRESS

"Joe Camp is a master storyteller." - *THE NEW YORK TIMES*

"Joe Camp is a natural when it comes to understanding how animals tick and a genius at telling us their story. His books are must-reads for those who love animals of any species." - *MONTY ROBERTS, AUTHOR OF NEW YORK TIMES BEST-SELLER THE MAN WHO LISTENS TO HORSES*

"Camp has become something of a master at telling us what can be learned from animals, in this case specifically horses, without making us realize we have been educated, and, that is, perhaps, the mark of a real teacher. The tightly written, simply designed, and powerfully drawn chapters often read like short stories that flow from the heart." - *JACK L. KENNEDY, THE JOPLIN INDEPENDENT*

"One cannot help but be touched by Camp's love and sympathy for animals and by his eloquence on the subject." - *MICHAEL KORDA, THE WASHINGTON POST*

"Joe Camp is a gifted storyteller and the results are magical. Joe entertains, educates and empowers, baring his own soul while articulating keystone principles of a modern revolution in horsemanship." - *RICK LAMB, AUTHOR AND TV/RADIO HOST "THE HORSE SHOW"*

For Kathleen, who loved me enough to initiate all this
when she was secretly terrified of horses

CONTENTS

I tell our horses:
You do something I like and I'll do something you like.

INTRODUCTION

Often, in the early evening, when the stresses of the day are weighing heavy, I pack it in and head out to the pasture. I'll sit on my favorite rock, or just stand, with my shoulders slumped, head down, and wait. It's never long before I feel the magical tickle of whiskers against my neck, or the elixir of warm breath across my ear, a restoring rub against my cheek. I have spoken their language and they have responded. And my problems have vanished. This book is written for everyone who has never experienced this miracle.

- Joe Camp
The Soul of a Horse
Life Lessons from the Herd

FOREWORD

I'm not a professional trainer. I do not do it for a living. But I am a student of what works. Logic and common sense to a fault, I suppose. The purpose of this book is to provide our discoveries to folks who love their horses and want to give them an environment in which there can be real communication, understanding, structure, compassion, growth, and trust.

And vocabulary.

Yes *vocabulary*!

Horses can learn the meanings of words and, like children, as their vocabulary grows they can put those words together into differing phrases and sentences. That's not supposed to be true according to most, but Kathleen and I have found it to be absolutely true. And now there is even a scientific study proving it, discussed later in this book.

But why would we fly in the face of virtually every trainer I've ever been exposed to who are all in lock step on the subject of treats. *Use them minimally, and never as a training device* they say in unison. But we have found that once your horse fully trusts you, of his own free will, and your relationship is in place, there is virtually nothing that horse won't do for you... *if* he *understands* what you're asking him to do. And that's a big *if* in too many instances. So communication is the key to training. Come on, say it with me: *Communication is the key to training*.

And when we discovered that training with treats not only made communication virtually guaranteed, for the first time it gave our horses a way for them to speak to us, to initiate conversation... that's when everything changed. With traditional training, *we* are always the ones doing the talking. Telling the horse, one way or another, to do this or do that. Never do we ask or listen to what the horse might want. And for the most part we teach with negative reinforcement. Release of pressure. In other words we stop doing something that is uncomfortable for the horse when he does something we'd like him to do. And we call it a reward.

Positive reinforcement would be something that the horse considers... well, positive. Good. Desired. Even fun.

Whoa! Hold on there. Have we stumbled onto something that actually teaches the horse and the horse enjoys it, thinks it's fun?

Yes, we did.

And that's what this book is all about.

1

IS IT FUN?

When I first walked Cash down to the arena to look at this new object, he stopped cold in his tracks and just gaped at it.

There was nothing in his memory banks that looked like this.

Then a breeze wafted by and the darn thing moved.

Oh my God, it's alive!

The next thing I knew Cash was at the other end of the arena, huffing and puffing. No idea how he got there. Seriously. None.

"It's just a circus ball," I hollered.

The look he gave me spoke volumes. But this circus ball and Cash would soon change my mind about a lot of things I needed to relearn.

Imagine an indoor arena. Twelve thousand wildly screaming fans there to see the season opener of a brand-new professional arena-football league. Music blaring. Drums pounding. Feet stomping. Spotlights undulating.

The perfect atmosphere for a horse, right?

At the time, I couldn't imagine taking one of ours into that fray. And yet Hasan, a majestic gray Arabian stallion, would gallop down a smoke-filled tunnel and out into this chaos, running right through a large rubber blow-up football helmet. The racket would escalate. Fireworks would explode into light and thunder as Hasan galloped around the arena. He would then rear and execute a hind-leg walk with his front legs landing perfectly on a pedestal upon which he would pivot in a complete circle, saluting all the fans with his right front leg. He would then stand motionless while a rumbling procession of motorcycles roared out of the inflatable helmet and circled him, delivering cheerleaders in short skirts to the field.

Even more clamor.

And Hasan just stood there!

Motionless. Relaxed.

As if nothing whatsoever was happening!

I couldn't believe it.

And it all started with a circus ball.

And a treat.

Hasan's trainer and constant companion of seventeen years is Allen Pogue. Allen's work has cast him as a trick trainer but the word *trick* does not even scratch the surface and seems to diminish the value to me. What he accomplishes for the horse is so much more than tricks. We're dumbfounded by how his horses treat him, and try for him. And have fun doing it.

Fun is a key word here because once basic natural training - what I call *leadership* training - of a horse has begun in earnest, after the horse has been given the choice of whether or not to trust you, to be in relationship with you, the work is all about maintaining leadership and relationship. But the repetition can become boring for owner and horse. Allen Pogue's training of self-motivated behaviors is all about removing the boredom, engaging the brain, and having fun. And communication is no longer a one-way street because the horse can now do something on his own that will speak to you.

According to Allen, the typical ranch horse or performance horse does not do much reasoning because he's never asked to. So much typical training is based on the horse's genetic desire to be safe and comfortable that the usual learning process is heavily slanted toward giving the horse the choice of either doing the behavior or being uncomfortable. It's called negative reinforcement. Like the simple request asking the horse to lower his head. It's either lower it, or feel the discomfort of halter pressure on top of your head.

I'll take the comfortable route, thank you very much.

The horse learns. There's no pain or cruelty. But not much reasoning either. And not a whole a lot of fun.

Which is why Allen's methods are so amazing.

At no other time, other than perhaps a frolic in the pasture, do we ever get to see the horse *having fun*. Especially while his brain is engaged and he's learning.

Fun?

What's that about?

Most folks grow up assuming that the horse's capacity to reason and his ability to have *fun* are just not part of his genetic make up. And unfortunately those subjects just never come up.

Didn't with us.

We never really thought about it. I was so focused on becoming one of the herd, using their language, directing them away from the reactive side of their brain, teaching them to move their various body parts – all of which is absolutely necessary to establishing a positive relationship with the horse, and necessary to clearly establishing my leadership role, which in the herd is based upon who moves who - that it just didn't occur to me that a horse could reason, much like a dog can reason. Or that the horse could develop a verbal vocabulary, like Benji. The caveat is that all the basic training must come first, because neither reasoning nor vocabulary will occur unless the horse trusts you enough to stay on the thinking side of his brain, and respects you enough to choose you as a herd leader. So please understand that everything that follows is predicated upon good, sound basic ground work that clearly establishes Trust and Relationship First and Leadership next.

Without that there is no opportunity for communication in either language, his or ours. With or without vocabulary.

But why, I was scolding myself, especially after decades of experience with Benji, did it never occur to me to use verbal vocabulary, or to expect the horse to be capable of rational thought. It was frustrating that none of this bubbled up until I began to worry that I was boring our horses with repetition.

Was this another episode of following the crowd?

"I keep telling myself I'm a logical thinker," I said to Kathleen one evening when we were discussing it. "But I'm beginning to wonder."

"I don't believe we've ever heard a trainer or clinician use the word *reasoning* in reference to a horse," she said. "Not until Allen. And most clinicians we've seen advise against using verbal cues, and treats."

I was beginning to wonder why.

"Perhaps because the horse's language in the herd is mostly visual," she said.

"So are dogs in a pack, but Benji understands a huge vocabulary."

"Why do you worry so? The timing is perfect. You just said that everything we've done had to go before trick training."

"It's not *trick* training," I said. "It's self-motivated behavior."

She raised an eyebrow and I sulked off to the computer to read more about Allen. And to see if he sold circus balls. Something new for Cash to focus on. Variety. Something different.

Cash in particular needed this because he was so bright. I was teaching him to back through the arena gate, a fairly scary thing for most horses, because a horse's only visual blind spot lies directly behind him. In front, there's a small area, right between the eyes, where they cannot see when the object is very close – which is why it's significant when a horse allows you to rub him on his forehead. Allowing you to rub where he cannot see definitely means he trusts you. But directly behind him he can see nothing unless he turns around or swings his head to the rear. For that reason it has taken quite some time to train some of our horses to back through the open gate. It makes them really nervous. But, like rubbing on the forehead, the process is ultimately a good thing for them because once they finally relax and do it comfortably, they're telling me, O*kay, I trust you. I am no longer afraid that you will back me into a horse-eating fence.*

And the relationship takes a step up.

The second time I walked Cash up to the gate and began to move his butt around to back him through, he swung right around and backed through all by himself.

The *second* time!

Okay, I've got it. What next?

How about a circus ball?

Bring it on.

That's how I stumbled onto Allen Pogue's *Imagine A Horse.*

And learned that horses can have fun.

And can grow to understand words. Even sentences.

And are fully capable of reasoning.

And that the use of treats can seriously speed up communication and comprehension. And the fun.

It was like the moment when suddenly the curtains parted and I realized why horses should be barefoot. Another cold, wet rag in the face.

Another *duh.*

I've been encouraging people for years in talks and seminars to exercise their brains every day. Take 'em out for a jog. The brain, like any other part of the body, works better the more it's used. And the more it's used, the better it works.

And this amazing phenomenon is not exclusive to humans.

Yet another epiphany.

The horse is a flight animal. Engaging his brain could be even more important to his ability to focus and reason than ours. It helps him control his own reactive side. Like Hasan did in that boisterous, explosive indoor arena setting.

"Please, Mr. Camp. I can't print that. Animals can't reason."

It was a reporter for the *Dallas Morning News* doing a story about the filming of the original *Benji* movie.

I was astonished. I had just spent thirty minutes ranting giddily about the unique concept of a dog *acting*, about the incredible facial expressions Benji was giving us, about those big brown eyes and the reams of dialogue they were speaking, about the dog himself and how for the first time I had come to realize that the story we were telling wasn't purely the emotional petition I had once thought but, in reality, quite plausible. Dogs, I had discovered, *can* think rationally. Can reason. And this particular one was extraordinary.

Not that other dogs aren't. Or horses. Or birds.

But most animals who have the intelligence, attitude and temperament to do what Benji was doing never have the opportunity to learn and to gain the vocabulary that Benji has.

"Vocabulary? That's ridiculous!"

I bit my tongue because we were on the air. This was later, a radio talk show in Norfolk, Virginia.

But Norfolk radio notwithstanding, Benji does have a vocabulary. And now I was beginning to realize that Cash could have one as well. He could think, and he could understand concepts. Just like Benji. Concepts like *other*. If you ask Benji for a foot, then ask for the *other* foot, she switches (yes, only the original Benji was a male). If she walks off toward a chair and is told to go to the *other* chair, she looks back to see *which* one, then takes the point and heads in that direction. She understands the concept of words like *slow, hurry, easy, go on,* and *not,* no matter how the words are applied. When asked to perform a difficult task, you can actually witness the process as she studies the situation to determine the best approach.

But none of this is particularly unusual. Sheepdogs in Europe tend entire flocks *by themselves* for months, keeping the sheep together, deciding when to move them from one pasture to another, even stopping the flock to check for vehicles before crossing a road.

I read about a horse who was taught to bring a small herd of cattle in from the pasture every week and put them in a pen for a screw worm checkup. He would do this religiously, completely on his own. After a few weeks he decided, again completely on his own, that it was quite a bit easier just to keep them in the pen than to have to go fetch them every week. So he did just that, refusing to let them out.

At a press conference in a Miami hotel suite, a dozen reporters watched the original Benji perform one of his standard show routines, completely unaware at the time that he had made a mess of it and would've never finished had he not been able to reason it through.

He was wedged between two banister poles, pulling a coffee mug tied to a string of leashes up to the mezzanine level which overlooked the group below. A person, of course, would use two hands, one over the other, but Benji used his mouth and a foot. He would reach down and pull up a length, hold it tightly against the floor with his foot, then reach down again and pull up another length, hold it with his foot, and so on, until he had retrieved whatever was tied to the other end. As he performed on this particular day, the leash slipped over the corner of the mezzanine floor and, because he was so snugly wedged between the banister poles, he could no longer reach it with the foot he had always used to hold it. I marveled as I watched the wheels turn. He pondered the situation for only a few seconds before he, quite logically, placed the *other* foot on the rope -- the foot he had *never* before used to hold it -- and went on with the routine as if nothing had happened.

Benji even understands what he's doing when he's acting.

"Now you've heard it all, folks. The dog understands he's acting! I suppose he gets script approval!"

Chicago. Another talk show host.

One of the more important sequences in the original Benji movie involved Benji moping forlornly through town. He knew that children were in danger but he was unable to communicate what he knew to the family, who had, in fact, scolded him for trying. For the sequence to work, indeed for the entire *story* to work, these scenes had to generate unencumbered empathy and support for Benji's plight. He had to look as if he had lost his last friend. His desperation had to reach out from those big brown eyes and squeeze passionately upon the hearts of the audience.

It worked so well that during the first rehearsal, I almost aborted the sequence. I was forty feet above the scene with the cameraman and camera in the bucket of a cherry picker -- the kind utility companies use to fix power lines -- and Frank Inn, Benji's trainer, was in the alley below *screaming* at Benji, "*Shame on you! Put your head down! Shame, shame on you!*"

Benji looked as if he had, *in fact*, lost his last friend. It was perfect. I *believed* him. But I couldn't bear to see him hurt so from the scolding.

I asked to be lowered back to the ground and I walked into the scene and asked Frank to hold for a minute while we talked.

"What's the matter?" he asked, eyes wide and curious. "Isn't this the look you want?"

"It's perfect," I said. "But I don't feel right about getting it this way."

"What the hell are you talking about?"

"I don't feel right about you scolding Benji like that."

Frank's eyes rolled heavenward. "Turn around," he said. "Does that look like a scolded dog?"

Benji was aimlessly scratching his ear. He looked up at me and yawned idly.

"Watch closely," said Frank. He motioned Benji onto his feet and began scolding him again. Our floppy-eared star's head dropped like a rock, his eyes drooped, and he looked as pitiful as anything I had ever seen. Then Frank relaxed, chirped a simple "Okay," and as if he had flipped an emotional switch, Benji blinked away the blues, had a good shake, wagged his tail, and awaited his next command. He fully understood what was going on, and scolding wasn't it. He might not have known the word, but he was, in the truest sense, acting.

He picked things up so quickly that he even astonished Frank on occasion. Like the time we realized he had deciphered what the word *cut* meant. We were all on the floor, crunched around the camera, down at Benji's eye level. When the shot was over, Frank began to unravel from the pile and suddenly realized his dog was nowhere in sight. "Your dog's no fool," one of the crew chuckled. "When Joe said, 'Cut,' he split for the air-conditioning."

Benji learned very quickly that the air conditioner was *his*. It was used to keep him from panting so that's where he was supposed to be when the camera wasn't rolling.

But telling these stories, and a dozen others like them, left not the slightest dent in the armor of the *Dallas Morning News* reporter covering the newly emerging film production scene in north Texas. The story came out the next day, on the front page. It was all about a seven-year-old Dallas girl and a nine-year-old Dallas boy making their motion picture debuts. The dog was barely mentioned. And there was certainly nothing about his ability to think. Or to reason.

Animals can't do that.

Not dogs. Not horses.

But don't tell that to Allen Pogue. He won't believe you. And he'll probably tell you this story about his mare Hasana.

"Whenever it was time for our young horses to be introduced to Liberty training – running free in a round pen without a line or lead rope - Hasana would be put in the ring with them, and she would help keep them in their assigned places in the lineup much better than any human handler could possibly do. If one got out of his place, as Gater would often do, she would trot right up alongside of him and promptly push him back into the lineup. If he resisted, she would become more insistent and give him the bossy mare look or a nip until he resigned himself to his job. The precision and understanding that she displayed in this responsibility was amazing and her ability to teach other horses was a considerable help to me."

Many trainers, if not most, do not agree with Allen on the use of treats. And, as mentioned, most eschew the use of verbal cues. But Allen uses words and treats to build brain power, relationship, communication, and fun. And, as they say about truth, when you see the results, the value is self-evident.

Kathleen notwithstanding, I like to call Allen's methods self-motivated behaviors because the horse chooses, on his own, to do it, or not. And there's no discomfort if he chooses not to.

It's worth repeating that a good relationship based upon choice, trust, respect, and leadership needs to be in place before training with treats is introduced (see Monty Roberts' Join Up links in the Resources section at the end of the book). Or the horse needs to be started very young, as Allen does now with all of his foals. Otherwise, many horses – and owners - can become treat crazy, which is neither good for the horse nor the owner. Once a horse is listening, his brain engaged, a bit of treat here and there, given at just the right time in response to something well done, can actually encourage listening, and reasoning. And truly speed up communication. I've found with ours that every one of them are anxious to figure out what I am requesting that they do. Traditional methods often turns into a sort of trial and error effort. I've heard many a clinician say, "Just keep applying the pressure and the horse will try all sorts of things trying to figure it out. Release the pressure immediately when he hits the correct answer."

How much easier it is to use vocabulary that he already knows and a well-placed treat. Cash does his flexing exercises without a halter or lead rope. And he learned to bow in about six minutes. More on that later.

Wouldn't it to be nice to walk into a pasture of six horses, call out to a horse by name, and have one horse look up? The right horse?

Or be able to merely say, "Lower your head, please." And have it happen.

Or have a horse come to greet you with a big, open mouthed smile? That's the first of Allen's behaviors that I began teaching Cash. Actually it looks more like a tooth-and-gum-showing pucker to me. As if the horse were offering a big sloppy kiss.

Horses use their soft floppy lips to sort through things, to check things out, to groom, to push away the dirt on a single strand of hay, or to tickle open your fingers to get to a treat. Which is the way the cued *smile* begins. As Cash's lips tickle my fingers, I raise my hand into the air, flip up my index finger, and say, "Smile." Cash had this down in no time. Even I was amazed. Now I need only to raise my hand and flick the index finger a couple of times and his lips open wide in an exaggerated goldfish pucker. And he holds it until I lower my hand.

He often offers the smile without my asking. Instead of the typical pushy, horsey-treat behavior, like shoving against you trying to get into a pocket, Cash walks up and smiles.

May I have a treat please?

"Absolutely," says I.

Deep into the first hour of teaching circus-ball nudging in the round pen, I decided to give us both a short break. I walked across to the far side of the pen and just leaned on the fence, arms draped across the top rail. Cash stood in place, maybe three or four feet away from the ball, and watched me until I was once again looking at him. Then he turned to the ball, took two steps, and nudged it not once, not twice, not three times, but four times, moving it a good ten or twelve feet. Then he turned back to me with that familiar cocked-head question of a look that asked: *Is that worth a paycheck?*

I laughed so hard I could hardly muster a "good boy."

He got his treat.

And because he was actually having fun, I got mine.

You do something I like and I'll do something you like.

Nobody ever gets a treat just because they're cute, or because I love them. It's always:

You do something I like and I'll do something you like.

A few days later we were actually playing "pitch and catch." I would roll the ball to him, and he would roll it back. How cool is that?

Thanks Allen for continuing our amazing journey of discovery. Our horses owe you.

As do we.

See Allen's website link in the Resources section at the end of this book.

2

CERTIFIED

A new scientific study reported by Discovery News verifies that horses are closer to people who treat them well. The study also praises the use of treats and words. Those who have read *The Soul of a Horse* or the first chapter of this book understand why that gets a big *Yippee!* from me. We have known for some time that these findings regarding treats and words are true but so many folks preach "Never use treats" and even "Don't talk to your horse" that's it's really nice to hear that what you believe and have proven to yourself to be true has finally been certified in a scientific manner. Now official so to speak. I immediately told Cash about it.

The study strongly verifies that horses are not only closer to people who treat them well, they are more willing, and remember them positively forever. Even after long separations.

Yes!

Trust and Relationship first!

The text of the article follows. It's a good read and super reinforcement for those of you who knew it all along but have grown tired of the hammering from naysayers:

Horses not only remember people who have treated them well, they also understand words better than expected, research shows - By Jennifer Viegas

Human friends may come and go, but a horse could be one of your most loyal, long-term buddies if you treat it right, suggests a new study.

Horses also understand words better than expected, according to the research, and possess "excellent memories," allowing horses to not only recall their human friends after periods of separation, but also to remember complex, problem solving strategies for ten years or more.

The bond with humans likely is an extension of horse behavior in the wild, since horses value their own horse relatives and friends, and are also open to new, non-threatening acquaintances.

"Horses maintain long-term bonds with several members of their family group, but they also interact temporarily with members of other groups when forming herds," explained Carol Sankey, who led the research, and her team.

"Equid social relationships are long-lasting and, in some cases, lifelong," added the scientists, whose paper has been accepted for publication in the journal *Animal Behavior*.

Ethologist Sankey of the University of Rennes and her colleagues studied 20 Anglo-Arabian and three French Saddlebred horses stabled in Chamberet, France. The scientists tested how well the horses remembered a female trainer and her instructions after she and the horses had been separated up to eight months.

The training program for the horses consisted of 41 steps associated with basic grooming and medical care. For example, the horses had to remain immobile in response to the verbal command "reste!" which is

French for "stay." The horses also had to lift their feet, tolerate a thermometer inserted into the rectum and more. When a horse did as it was instructed, the trainer rewarded it with food pellets.

With tasty rewards, the horses "displayed more 'positive' behaviors toward the experimenter, such as sniffing and licking," the researchers wrote. Horses do this as a sign of affiliation with each other, so they weren't necessarily just seeking more food.

The scientists added, "Horses trained without reinforcement expressed four to six times more 'negative' behaviors, such as biting, kicking and 'falling down' on the experimenter."

Nevertheless, after the eight months of separation, the horses trained with food rewards gravitated towards the same experimenter. The horses also seemed to accept new people more readily, indicating they had developed a "positive memory of humans" in general.

"From our results, it appears that horses are no different than humans (in terms of positive reinforcement teachings)," according to the researchers. "They behave, learn and memorize better when learning is associated with a positive situation."

While people often train dogs in this way, also using verbal commands, Sankey and her team point out that "the majority of horseriding training is based on tactile sensations — pressure from bits, movements of riders' legs, weight change in the saddle."

Since "horses are able to learn and memorize human words" and can hear the human voice better than even dogs can, due to their particular range of hearing, the scientists predict trainers could have success if they incorporate more vocal commands into their horse training programs.

3

ASKING POLITELY

"Give me your foot."

"No, no, your *other* foot."

As mentioned earlier Benji is taught to understand concepts. Like the concept of *other*.

First, of course, she is taught to understand what her foot is. But that's immediately followed with the concept of *other*. Because, once understood, it can be used in so many ways.

"Go to the chair."

"No, the other chair."

And so on.

When we're doing demonstrations with Benji I always do the foot thing early on to show off how well she understands the concept.

Shortly after being introduced to treat-training with horses by Allen Pogue it occurred to me that it might be cute to have our little bitty Benji standing next to our great big Cash, each offering their feet simultaneously.

"Give me your foot."

And both horse and dog would lift a foot.

"No, no. Your *other* foot."

And both horse and dog would switch.

I didn't really think we'd ever really have the opportunity to use it but I liked the idea of teaching Cash the concept now that I firmly believed he was thoroughly capable of learning and applying the lesson. Can you imagine how much easier it would be to communicate with a horse who has a vocabulary and can actually think?

I began the process not unlike Benji's training had begun by pointing out to Cash what the word *foot* actually means, and what action I was asking for. I put my hand behind his knee and lifted his leg into sort of a Spanish walk position. All the while saying, "Your foot, your foot" over and over. Then I'd say "Good boy" and give him a treat while still holding his leg up. Only then would I lower his foot back the ground.

Side note: we use Omega Fields' *Omega Nibblers Low Sugar & Starch* treats, the only treat I've found on the planet that is actually *good* for the horse. They are great tasting and a functional source of plant derived Omega 3 with the best ratios of natural Omega 9 and Omega 6, made from human grade Non-GMO 99.9% pure stabilized ground flaxseed and natural ingredients. No sugar or molasses, no corn or other grains that turn to sugar immediately upon entering the body, and no soy. With an extremely low NSC of 14.1. This is an amazing treat! Omega Fields recommends 15 treats a day as an Omega 3 supplement so I never feel guilty or worried about over-training.

It didn't take Cash long to understand that when I said "Your foot. Give me your foot" that I was asking him to lift it off the ground. In very short order I was no longer lifting the leg, but merely touching his knee and he would lift it up himself. And soon after that all I needed were the words and a bit of hand motion. It was fun to watch his comprehension unfold, very similar to Benji's.

Maybe it's just because I've grown up with a dog training mentality, but frankly I wouldn't know where to start if I were to attempt to teach this without the treat. Whatever route that might take I'm certain Cash would not have understood it so quickly. He wouldn't have grasped my communication so readily. Nor would he have been as motivated to reach, and understand, and do.

In other words he was enjoying the process and that made both of us happy. And lo and behold, he was also learning that when I asked for something new, something he had never done before, he'd get that brain engaged quickly because there might be something good in it for him. He was seriously focused on figuring it out.

When he reached the point of offering his foot every time I asked for it, I switched to the "other" side and began to reinforce the concept of *other*. I switched hands - exactly as I would've done if I were working with Benji – so he would have a visual, physical difference to associate with the word *other* (which eventually is no longer necessary once the meaning of the word is absorbed). I would lift the right leg - as I had done with the left leg - saying over and over, "Your *other* foot. Now give me your *other* foot." This concept, being a bit more complex, came to him more slowly. But not as slowly as I anticipated.

Late in the afternoon the very day I had begun working on Cash's "other" side, Kathleen drifted down to the tack room area, under what we referred to as our covered bridge, where we would often sit on the tack room steps and catch up with each other's day. Cash had not yet processed all the new information to a point where he would lift his right foot without assistance.

As Kathleen and I chatted, Cash just hung out, as he often did during these sessions. Suddenly Kathleen broke into a chuckle.

"I think your boy wants something," she grinned.

I turned to Cash and he was all teeth, wearing a huge well-executed smile.

Might I have a treat please?"

Kathleen has always said that if Cash ever spoke out loud it would surely be with a British accent because he was so polite, so very much a gentleman.

"No," I said to him. "I told you we're done with treats for today."

I turned back to Kathleen but her eyes were on Cash, not me. And her smile was stretching from ear to ear.

"I don't think so," she said.

I glanced over my shoulder and Cash was lifting his left foot and lightly pawing the air.

He made me laugh so I'm very sure he knew he was winning.

"No!" I said, trying to sound firm without much success. "We're done with treats for the day. Done. Fini!"

Back to Kathleen.

"What's he doing now?" I asked.

"Oh my," Kathleen gulped. "I thought you said he didn't have the *other* foot thing down yet."

I spun around and Cash was pawing the air… with his *right* foot, his *other* foot. Kathleen was laughing out loud. And now so was I. He knew he had us. You could read it in his eyes. And I could no longer help myself. I reached for the treat bag.

But how cool is that?

I mean seriously. He figured all that out himself, including the "other" foot which he had never before actually offered to me. He was saying as politely as you could imagine:

Please! Just one more?

How could I refuse?

Now we have a routine that we follow in such situations, when Cash asks for yet another treat. Remember back in the Foreword I mentioned that words, once learned, can be linked together in different ways, different phrases, even sentences. Actual conversations. This is a terrific example of just that. Say we're wrapping up a session and Cash lays his big toothy smile on me.

Just one more treat. Puleeze!

I'll usually harrumph a bit, and then say:

"Oh...alright. Just *one* more. Okay? Just... *one*... more."

Another big smile.

I give him a treat.

And he actually turns and walks away.

Conversation over.

And it always leaves me smiling.

The first few times we did this I had to shoo him away but he very quickly linked the words to the action. He fully understands that when I say *just one more*, that's it. He's supposed to walk away. He totally gets it.

Our training sessions are not really "training" sessions as such. They're just snippets of time right before mixing the morning and evening feed. At liberty, out behind the barn. These are the only times I ever seem to steal a few minutes to work with any of the horses. During those brief sessions Cash has learned the following:

Make a bow

This began by holding the treat between his legs while saying, "Make a bow. Come on, make a bow." With each succession, the hand holding the treat would get lower and lower until his nose was almost touching the ground. Then he'd get the treat. As soon as I felt he sort of understood the words, I no longer fed the treat from the cuing hand, but stood up saying, "Good boy!" then I'd give him the treat from the other hand. Soon I was able to move the hand cue to merely a touch under his arm pit (leg pit?). Later I began to bow *with* him (above), and that, along with the words, became the cue. Now if I make a bow either by his side or facing him he will bow with me, with or without the words. So the routine became the two of us side by side making a bow together as if to an audience.

Then I move out in front to face him and we bow to each other. Very cute.

Usually I'll give him a treat and a "Good boy" after the two bows. But not always. Sometimes we'll do three or four things before he gets one treat. I've started stretching the distance when I face him and we've done the bow to each other as far apart as 12-15 feet.

Say hello

I wave at him, using the words, "Say hello," and he lifts his leg and paws the air. Then I wave again and say "Now, the other foot. Say hello." and he "waves" with the other foot. Both, of course, are mere extensions of the earlier *Give me your foot* lesson. As a side note, occasionally Cash gets lazy and doesn't lift his foot high enough so I began to use an upward hand gesture, saying, "No. Up! Up, up, up!" and it didn't take long at all for him to grasp the concept. Now he understands "up" if his head is too low when flexing, or if his smile is not high enough, or if he anticipates a bow before I ask for it. And he also knows the word "down" which is used to ask him to lower his head.

Flex

One of the first exercises we teach a new horse in the round pen is to flex his head laterally all the away around until he is touching his rib cage. On both sides. We teach this using a halter and a lead rope, doing it over and over again until the horse flexes with virtually no pressure on the line at all. The purpose: it softens the horse in the neck and shoulders and, most importantly, the exercise is continued when in the saddle and it becomes so automatic to the horse that we now have a one-rein stop that doesn't turn into a tug of war with a beastie six to eight times our size. An emergency brake so to speak.

One day I was playing with Cash and wondered if he would flex at liberty, without the halter and lead rope. It took less than sixty seconds for him to grasp the concept using treats and words. I would hold the treat back against his rib cage saying, "Flex, Cash" and when he touched his side I'd give it to him. As soon as he got the picture, the cue became just a finger touch on his side with the word *flex*. And a treat after. When I went to the other side I used the words "Now the other side. Flex, Cash."

That transitioned into merely reaching across his back to touch the "other" side, saying "Now the *other* side Cash. Flex. The *other* side." And he does.

Smile

This was the first thing I taught Cash using treats, and is the first thing I teach every horse. It's so fast and easy, and quickly sets up the concept that *If you do something I like, I'll do something you like.* All of our horses do the smile. But teaching each one was a little different. Start with a treat grasped loosely in your closed hand, fingers facing the horse, up not down. Place your hand at about your own eye level. Let the horse smell that you have a treat. Say the word *smile* over and over. *Big smile.* Some horses need no more than this and will begin to "lip" your hand, opening their lips as they would when separating a piece of grass or hay. But don't give the treat until the horse seriously lifts that upper lip way up. If that doesn't happen begin to wiggle your index finger, sort of tickling the upper lip. This will help cause that upper lip to reach upward. And this finger movement will become your visual cue. A quick point and upward wiggle of the index finger. With the word *smile*. I can now get a smile from Cash from 10-15 feet away using the verbal and finger cue.

Whenever your horse does correctly, give him an immediate "Good boy" plus the treat you hold in your hand. Some horses need to be tickled harder than others. With one, I had to reach out and actually lift the upper lip into smiling position before he understood.

Now that Cash understands the word "up" I use that verbal cue to get his head or lip higher if necessary.

Whoa!

Cash is Polish Arab and for the longest time I was writing off his anxiousness under saddle to "just being Arab." Most of that went away when we changed to bitless. He was a different horse. Much more relaxed. Listening better. Softer. But he had never really grasped the concept of stopping with only the butt cue, me sitting back, relaxing my weight toward the rear. Both Kathleen and I wanted to perfect this stop because we both prefer leg and body cues to reins. Clinicians preach that if he doesn't stop when you sit back and say *whoa* then pull him immediately into a series of tight circles, each one getting ever smaller until he finally stops. Then release the reins. Do this every time he doesn't stop, until finally he gets tired of making tight circles and decides it's better to just stop in the first place. But that never happened with Cash. It was probably my fault because my heart wasn't in the method I had been told to use. It reminded me of those who physically dominate the horse to get submission, only this was more mental than physical domination. Yet it never seemed that Cash connected the two. Tight circles and not stopping. And I refused to get more aggressive with him.

One day I thought why not try a treat to get the point across. See if he was being ornery or if it was really a communication problem. A concept he didn't understand. We did a bunch of stops using the "sit back" along with slight pressure on the (bitless) reins. He would stop, but drift forward a couple of steps. I added the word *whoa* to the drill and finally he nailed it. Stopped on a dime. Immediately I praised him with lots of *good boys* and rubs... and a treat. He reached back, took it... and that was that. Done. The next few stops were all perfect. And he got a treat after each one. Then a treat after every other stop. Then after every third stop. And so it went until the treats became every rare once in a while.

And the concept was locked in. There hasn't been an issue with stopping since that day. He totally understands the gig. And he's happy to do it. It was as if he said *Oh! I get it! That sloppy sit-back you're doing means stop. Okay. Now I understand.*

Walk with Me

Twice every day when I go down to feed I'm faced with
sorting out the horses to their respective feeding sta-
tions. Sometimes it takes no effort at all and other
times it's fruit-basket-turnover depending on who's
where, their individual moods, the weather, and whatever else is going on. If, for example, they're all hanging
out in the front paddock of the barn, then five of them
have to be "relocated" before feeding can start because
Noelle, the mustang and herd leader, is fed in the round
pen to keep her from stealing everyone else's food. Each

horse is fed in a specific place, determined by his or her dominance position in the herd and how fast or slowly they eat, but sorting them into those places is often… hmmm… interesting. When we first moved to middle Tennessee I usually had to use halters to lead this horse that way and that horse this way. But a few weeks of that was quite enough. I decided to teach each horse to "walk with me" at liberty.

Wherever I wanted to go.

Whichever direction.

And however far.

A pretty cool thing when you think about the complexity of communicating this objective to the horse. A horse who is not alone with you in some arena but has every possible distraction available, other horses, grass, weeds, whatever. But it worked. And the hero was the treat each horse received at the end of the walk. That kept them focused, and looking forward. The process began by urging just a couple of steps with the words, "Walk with me." Rewarded by a treat. Then a few more steps. And finally walking to wherever I needed to take them. It blows most visitors away when I walk into the paddock and have horses come right up and say *where are we walking to tonight?* And then follow me off, very politely, through the round pen, or out into the western pasture, or through the barn into the rear paddock.

Every communication I've tried with any of our horses has shown better results faster using treats and words. So I admit it was nice to stumble upon the study detailed in the previous chapter. It made my day.

Mouse, who, like Cash, is extremely bright, has learned to step up onto Malachi's little platform and turn 360-degree circles without slipping off.

Mouse stepping up

She begins the turn

Half way around – following the treat

She knew right from the beginning that once she was on the platform her feet were supposed to stay there. When one would slip off she would quickly put it right back on. She learned the entire circle in just a couple of sessions. Now she climbs up on her own and looks around for me. *Well come on. Let's do this circle thing.*

As mentioned earlier, all our horses smile, and Skeeter, Mouse, and Mariah are learning to bow. All using treats.

Mouse reaches for the treat between her legs

The treat is a positive reinforcement. The horse receives something he or she likes in return for understanding and doing what you want, so it all becomes fun. And enhances your relationship. And gives them a way to initiate a conversation with you.

Yet negative reinforcement is still the norm for training horses. "Make the right thing easy and the wrong thing difficult." Or "Make the right thing comfortable and the wrong thing uncomfortable." Either way it's teaching via negative reinforcement. The horse gets nothing for doing what you would like him to do except relief from something negative. Something he doesn't like.

Do be careful. Be cautious. Think your way through all this with your horses. Our horses never get treats just because they're there. Just because we love them. Every treat given is as a response to them doing something we are asking for. *You do something I like and I'll do something you like.* Okay, maybe they use what they have learned to politely ask sometimes. And yes, it often works. But not one of them has ever turned into a treat hound. And please don't start training with treats until your relationship is right, until the horse has chosen you to be his trusted leader by you giving him the opportunity to make that choice completely on his own. And until you have lived up to that leadership role. This means working from the horse's end of the lead rope first. Understanding and using his language, and the way his herd dynamics work. See *Relationship First* and *Leadership Second* on our website thesoulofahorse.com.

Only then should you offer him the opportunity to now understand *your* language. To play the way you play. To learn the way you learn. Only then can he feel

secure enough in his trust to truly embrace and understand these new ways and new things, and give himself
fully to the effort.

But if you follow the above order of things give
himself he will. And you'll both be happier for the experience.

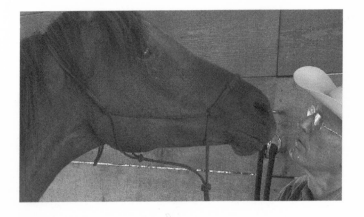

4

I've Been Told
My Standards Are Too High

I've heard that a lot.

You set your standards too high.

Can you imagine?

I've been searching for a treat that is actually good for my horses. A treat that isn't loaded with sugar or molasses, or grains which are mostly non-structural carbs which turn into sugar when metabolized, or soy, or hydrogenated vegetable fats or oils. As you well know by now we use a lot of treats. So I've been reading a lot of labels. Most of them are scary.

There is no such thing as a treat that is actually good for your horse. Get used to it.

That's a quote from someone who's supposed to know.

But that's not the way I believe. I've learned that when you dig deep enough, search long enough and question loudly enough, you'll discover the most amazing things. Things that will make for happier, healthier horses.

And find it I did!

Please turn the page.

A Treat That Is Actually Good For Your Horse!

From people who appear to actually care about your horse's health and happiness. This is the singular best treat on the market as far as I'm concerned because Omega Fields' *Omega Nibblers® Low Sugar & Starch* is the *only* treat I have found that uses 99.9% pure Non-GMO stabilized ground fortified flax. That's .9% higher than required for human food grade. Nobody else does this. Every heart-shaped treat contains 684mg of properly balanced Omega 3s, and 15 of these treats are a tasty Omega 3 alternative to a maintenance serving of *Omega Horseshine.*

Omega 3s are absolutely essential to your horse in so many ways! They fight inflammation, they support and build the immune system, improve bone and joint health, restore cracked and brittle hooves and support strong solid hoof growth, they can eliminate sweet itch and bug-bite sores, are recommended for horses with insulin resistance and Cushings, and can reduce symptoms of metabolic syndrome, all while promoting shiny, healthy coats and smoother skin texture! Our Stormy looks like she has been shellacked. Seriously. It's the shiniest winter coat I've ever seen. And the shine outside confirms the shine that's going on inside.

Every domestic horse on the planet needs Omega 3 supplementation because no one, horse or human, can manufacture their own Omega 3s. A horse in the wild will get his Omega 3 needs from the many varied kinds of fresh native grasses that have never been exposed to chemical fertilizers, pesticides, herbicides, and never been GMO'd. Domestic pastures virtually always come up short because they've been exposed to one or all of the above, and grass hay loses its Omega 3s when it is cut and dried, so the horse (like the human) needs Omega 3 supplementation.

But without molasses and/or grains with high levels of non-structural carbs that turn to sugar the minute they enter a horse's body (all grains have high NSCs). Like Corn or corn by-products, wheat or wheat middlings, barley, etc. Even carrots and carrot by-products carry a high glycemic index. Dr. Mark DePaolo, DVM says, "Horses are not designed to eat sugars or carbohydrates. ALL grains, when digested, are processed and metabolized as sugar which is detrimental to your horse's health and well-being." Also these sugars load up your horse with high doses of Omega 6, an inflammatory when not balanced properly with Omega 3.

And without soy. No Soybean meal or soybean oil. According to Dr. DePaolo, "Soy is highly estrogenic and should never be fed to either sex of horses, especially those that are already suffering from any type of metabolic disorder like Hypothyroidism, Insulin Resistance or Cushing's Syndrome. And 99.9% percent of soy included in human and horse food is genetically modified to be Round-Up Ready. Glyphosate, one of the active ingredients in Roundup, is the leading cause of leaky gut syndrome in horses. Leaky gut syndrome can cause food allergies, diarrhea, mal-absorption syndrome, colic and irritable bowel syndrome.

"Phytates in soy are also undesirable. They will bind to certain nutritional minerals in a horse's diet and prevent them from being absorbed into the body. It is very common for a horse that is being fed soy to be lacking Iron, Manganese, Chromium, Cobalt and sometimes Selenium when tested utilizing horse hair analysis. These minerals are very important in the production of proteinaceous connective tissues such as tendon, ligament, joint cartilage, hoof and hair coat."

Nibblers Low Sugar & Starch contain no hydrogenated vegetable fats or oils, all of which put high levels of unbalanced Omega 6s into your horse which cause free-radicals and inflammation when not balanced properly with Omega 3s.

If you are currently using another treat, I encourage you to check out the label. I have for every major treat out there. You will find no other brand using such a high quality flax. Many don't even use pure flax, opting for a less expensive and less effective flax by-product like *flax meal*. And you will find many treats filled with sugar, molasses, grains, soy and vegetable oils. Now read the ingredients for Omega Fields' *Omega Nibblers®️ Low Sugar* treats: *Stabilized Ground Flaxseed, Stabilized Rice Bran, Alfalfa Meal, Beet Pulp, Yeast Culture, Salt, Natural & Artificial Apple Flavor, Mixed Tocopherols (Natural Preservative).*

As mentioned earlier, once the horse has said *I trust you*, of his own free will with no strings attached, he will become a very willing partner. We have seven horses and every one of them will do anything in the world for us... *IF* they understand whatever it is we'd like for them to do... *IF* we can communicate that wish to them in a clear and intelligible manner. It's all about the *communication!* And I've never found a better way of confirming their understanding of communication than the concept of *You do something I like and I'll do something you like.*

And at last I need worry no longer about doing too much training and feeding too many treats.

Ever!

Check them out.

Thank you Omega Fields. The people who seriously care about my horse's health and happiness. - Joe Camp

Buy 'em - Try 'em - Save 10%
http://thesoulofahorse.com/omega-nibblers-ls-treat-flyer/

Buy three bags and get a free Kindle edition of
Training with Treats

(see next page)

Email your invoice number or numbers verifying your
purchase or purchases to
nancy@thesoulofahorse.com

Send along the email address where you want the
confirmation sent. Then you can have this book on all
your devices with Amazon's free kindle app.

*All the links in this book are live links in the
Amazon Kindle edition*

Watch these videos on:

The Soul of a Horse Channel on Vimeo
or
The Soul of a Horse Channel on YouTube

How to Catch Your Horse in the Pasture
All of this was taught using treats.

I Called Him… and He Came

Why The Soul of a Horse?

Born Wild
The Journey Continues

Miss Firestorm
Conceived in the Wild – Born to Us

Malachi
Our First Baby Conceived in the Wild

Benji Gets a New Baby… Horse

Follow Joe & Kathleen's Journey
From no horses and no clue to stumbling through mistakes, fear, fascination and frustration on a collision course with the ultimate discovery that something was very wrong in the world of horses.

Read the National Best Seller
The Soul of a Horse
Life Lessons from the Herd
http://thesoulofahorse.com

...and the highly acclaimed best selling sequel...

Born Wild
The Journey Continues
http://thesoulofahorse.com

What Critics Are Saying About Joe Camp

"Joe Camp is a master storyteller." *THE NEW YORK TIMES*

"Joe Camp is a gifted storyteller and the results are magical. Joe entertains, educates and empowers, baring his own soul while articulating keystone principles of a modern revolution in horsemanship." *RICK LAMB, AUTHOR AND TV/RADIO HOST "THE HORSE SHOW"*

"This book is fantastic. It has given me shivers, made me laugh and cry, and I just can't seem to put it down!" *CHERYL PANNIER, WHO RADIO AM 1040 DES MOINES*

"One cannot help but be touched by Camp's love and sympathy for animals and by his eloquence on the subject." *MICHAEL KORDA, THE WASHINGTON POST*

"Joe Camp is a natural when it comes to understanding how animals tick and a genius at telling us their story. His books are must-reads for those who love animals of any species." *MONTY ROBERTS, AUTHOR OF NEW YORK TIMES BEST-SELLER THE MAN WHO LISTENS TO HORSES*

"Camp has become something of a master at telling us what can be learned from animals, in this case specifically horses, without making us realize we have been educated, and, that is, perhaps, the mark of a real teacher. The tightly written, simply designed, and powerfully drawn chapters often read like short stories that flow from the heart." *JACK L. KENNEDY, THE JOPLIN INDEPENDENT*

Also by Joe Camp

The National Best Seller
The Soul of a Horse
Life Lessons from the Herd

The #1 Amazon Bestselling Sequel
Born Wild
The Soul of a Horse

#1 Amazon Bestseller
Horses & Stress
Eliminating the Root Cause of Most Health, Hoof & Behavior Problem

#1 Amazon Bestseller
Why Relationship First Works
Why and How It Changes Everything

#1 Amazon Bestseller
Beginning Ground Work
Everything We've Learned About Relationship and Leadership

Amazon Bestseller
Why Our Horses Are Barefoot
Everything We've Learned About the
Health and Happiness of the Hoof

God Only Knows
Can You Trust Him with the Secret?

The Soul of a Horse Blogged

Amazon Bestseller
Horses Were Born To Be On Grass
How We Discovered the Simple But Undeniable
Truth About Grass, Sugar, Equine Diet & Lifestyle

Horses Without Grass
How We Kept Six Horses Moving and Eating Happily
Healthily on an Acre and a Half of Rocks and Dirt

Dog On It
Everything You Need To Know About Life Is Right There At Your Feet

RESOURCES

There are, I'm certain, many programs and people who subscribe to these philosophies and are very good at what they do but are not listed in these resources. That's because we haven't experienced them, and we will only recommend to you programs that we believe, from our own personal experience, to be good for the horse and well worth the time and money.

https://www.imagineahorse.com- This is Allen Pogue and Suzanne De Laurentis' site. I cannot recommend strongly enough that everyone who leaves this book ready to take the next step with treats and vocabulary should visit this site and start collecting Allen's DVDs (he also sells big red circus balls). Because of his liberty work with multiple horses Allen has sort of been cast as a trick trainer, but he's so much more than that. It's all about relationship and foundation. We are dumbfounded by how Allen's horses treat him and try for him. His work with newborn foals and young horses is so logical and powerful that you should study it even if you never intend to own a horse. Allen says, "With my young horses, by the time they are three years old they are so mentally mature that saddling and riding is absolutely undramatic." He has taken Dr. Robert M. Miller's book *Imprint Training of the Newborn Foal* to a new and exponential level.

Monty Roberts and Join up:

http://www.montyroberts.com- Please start here! Or at Monty's Equus Online University which is terrific and probably the best Equine learning value out there on the internet (Watch the Join-Up lesson <u>and</u> the Special Event lesson. Inspiring!). This is where you get the relationship right with your horse. Where you learn to give him the choice of whether or not to trust you. Where everything changes when he does. Please, do this. Learn Monty's Join-Up method, either from his Online University, his books, or DVDs. Watching his *Join-Up* DVD was probably our single most pivotal experience in our very short journey with horses. Even if you've owned your horse forever, go back to the beginning and execute a Join Up with your horse or horses. You'll find that when you unconditionally offer choice to your horse and he chooses you, everything changes. You become a member of the herd, and your horse's leader, and with that goes responsibility on his part as well as yours. Even if you don't own horses, it is absolutely fascinating to watch Monty put a saddle and a rider on a completely unbroken horse in less than thirty minutes (unedited!). We've also watched and used Monty's *Dually Training Halter* DVD and his *Load-Up trailering* DVD. And we loved his books: *The Man Who Listens to Horses, The Horses in My Life, From My Hands to Yours, and Shy Boy.* Monty is a very impressive man who cares a great deal for horses.

Frederick Pignon – This man is amazing and has taken relationship and bond with his horses to an astounding new level. Go to this link: **http://www.youtube.com/watch?v=w1YO3j-Zh3g** and watch the video of his show with three beautiful black

Lusitano stallions, all at liberty. This show would border on the miraculous if they were all geldings, but they're not. They're stallions. Most of us will never achieve the level of bond Frederick has achieved with his horses but it's inspiring to know that it's possible, and to see what the horse-human relationship is capable of becoming. Frederick believes in true partnership with his horses, he believes in making every training session fun not work, he encourages the horses to offer their ideas, and he uses treats. When Kathleen read his book *Gallop to Freedom* her response to me was simply, "Can we just move in with them?"

<u>Natural Horsemanship</u>: This is the current buzz word for those who train horses or teach humans the training of horses without any use of fear, cruelty, threats, aggression, or pain. The philosophy is growing like wildfire, and why shouldn't it? If you can accomplish everything you could ever hope for with your horse and still have a terrific relationship with him or her, and be respected as a leader, not feared as a dominant predator, why wouldn't you? As with any broadly based general philosophy, there are many differing schools of thought on what is important and what isn't, what works well and what doesn't. Which of these works best for you, I believe, depends a great deal on how you learn, and how much reinforcement and structure you need. In our beginnings, we more or less shuffled together Monty Roberts (above) and the next two whose websites are listed below, favoring one source for this and another for that. But beginning with Monty's Join-Up. Often, this gave us an opportunity to see how different programs handle the same topic, which enriches insight. But, ultimately, they all end up at the same place:

When you have a good relationship with your horse that began with choice, when you are respected as your horse's leader, when you truly care for your horse, then, before too long, you will be able to figure out for yourself the best communication to evoke any particular objective. These programs, as written, or taped on DVD, merely give you a structured format to follow that will take you to that goal.

> http://www.parelli.com - Pat and Linda Parelli have turned their teaching methods into a fully accredited college curriculum. We have four of their home DVD courses: *Level 1, Level 2, Level 3,* and *Liberty & Horse Behavior.* We recommend them all, but especially the first three. Often, they do run on, dragging out points much longer than perhaps necessary, but we've found, particularly in the early days, that knowledge gained through such saturation always bubbles up to present itself at the most opportune moments. In other words, it's good. Soak it up. It'll pay dividends later. Linda is a good instructor, especially in the first three programs, and Pat is one of the most amazing horsemen I've ever seen. His antics are inspirational for me. Not that I will ever duplicate any of them, but knowing that it's possible is very affirming. And watching him with a newborn foal is just fantastic. The difficulty for us with *Liberty & Horse Behavior* (besides its price) is on disk 5 whereon Linda consumes almost three hours to load an inconsistent horse into a trailer. Her belief is that the horse should *not* be *made* to do anything, he should *discover* it on his own. I believe

there's another option. As Monty Roberts teaches, there is a big difference between *making* a horse do something and *leading* him through it, showing him that it's okay, that his trust in you is valid. Once you have joined up with him, and he trusts you, he is willing to take chances for you because of that trust, so long as you don't abuse the trust. On Monty's trailer-loading DVD Monty takes about one-tenth the time, and the horse (who was impossible to load before Monty) winds up loading himself from thirty feet away, happily, even playfully. And his trust in Monty has progressed as well, because he reached beyond his comfort zone and learned it was okay. His trust was confirmed. One thing the Parelli program stresses, in a way, is a followup to Monty Roberts' Join-Up: you should spend a lot of time just hanging out with your horse. In the stall, in the pasture, wherever. Quality time, so to speak. No agenda, just hanging out. Very much a relationship enhancer. And don't ever stomp straight over to your horse and slap on a halter. Wait. Let your horse come to you. It's that choice thing again, and Monty or Pat and Linda Parelli can teach you how it works.

http://www.chrislombard.com/ - An amazing horseman and wonderful teacher. His DVD *Beginning with the Horse* puts relationship, leadership and trust into simple easy-to-understand terms.

http://www.robertmmiller.com - Dr. Robert
M. Miller is an equine veterinarian and world
renowned speaker and author on horse behavior
and natural horsemanship. I think his name
comes up more often in these circles than any-
one else's. His first book, *Imprint Training of the
Newborn Foal* is now a bible of the horse world.
He's not really a trainer, per se, but a phenome-
nal resource on horse behavior. He will show
you the route to "the bond." You must visit his
website.

Taking Your Horse Barefoot: Taking your horses barefoot involves more than just pulling shoes. The new
breed of natural hoof care practitioners have studied
and rely completely on what they call the wild horse
trim, which replicates the trim that horses give to
themselves in the wild through natural wear. The more
the domesticated horse is out and about, moving constantly, the less trimming he or she will need. The more
stall-bound the horse, the more trimming will be needed in order to keep the hooves healthy and in shape.
Every horse is a candidate to live as nature intended.
The object is to maintain their hooves as if they were in
the wild, and that requires some study. Not a lot, but
definitely some. I now consider myself capable of keeping my horses' hooves in shape. I don't do their regular
trim, but I do perform interim touch-ups. The myth
that domesticated horses *must* wear shoes has been
proven to be pure hogwash. The fact that shoes degen-
erate the health of the hoof and the entire horse has not
only been proven, but is also recognized even by those
who nail shoes on horses. Successful high performance
barefootedness with the wild horse trim can be accom-

plished for virtually every horse on the planet, and the process has even been proven to be a healing procedure for horses with laminitis and founder. On this subject, I beg you not to wait. Dive into the material below and give your horse a longer, healthier, happier life.

> http://www.hoofrehab.com/– This is Pete Ramey's website. If you read only one book on this entire subject, read Pete's *Making Natural Hoof Care Work for You.* Or better yet, get his DVD series *Under the Horse,* which is fourteen-plus hours of terrific research, trimming, and information. He is my hero! He has had so much experience with making horses better. He cares so much about every horse that he helps. And all of this comes out in his writing and DVD series. If you've ever doubted the fact that horses do not need metal shoes and are in fact better off without them, please go to Pete's website. He will convince you otherwise. Then use his teachings to guide your horses' venture into barefootedness. He is never afraid or embarrassed to change his opinion on something as he learns more from his experiences. Pete's writings have also appeared in *Horse & Rider* and are on his website. He has taken all of Clinton Anderson's horses barefoot.

The following are other websites that contain good information regarding the barefoot subject:

http://www.TheHorsesHoof.com– this website and magazine of Yvonne and James Welz is de-

voted entirely to barefoot horses around the
world and is surely the single largest resource for
owners, trimmers, case histories, and virtually
everything you would ever want to know about
barefoot horses. With years and years of barefoot experience, Yvonne is an amazing resource.
She can compare intelligently this method vs
that and help you to understand all there is to
know. And James is a super barefoot trimmer.

https://www.facebook.com/eddie.drabek
This is the website of Eddie Drabek, another
one of my heroes. Eddie is a wonderful trimmer
in Houston, Texas, and an articulate and inspi-
rational educator and spokesman for getting
metal shoes off horses. Read everything he has
written, including the pieces on all the horses
whose lives he has saved by taking them barefoot.

Our current hoof specialist in Tennessee is
Mark Taylor who works in Tennessee, Arkan-
sas, Alabama, and Mississippi 662-224-4158
http:// http://www.natural-hoof.com/

See our Bare Feet section of **thesoulofa-
horse.com** including how and where to find a
recommended trimmer.

Also see: **the video of Joe: Why Are Our Horses Barefoot? On** The Soul of a Horse Channel on YouTube.

Natural Boarding: Once your horses are barefoot,
please begin to figure out how to keep them out around

the clock, day and night, moving constantly, or at least having that option. It's really not as difficult as you might imagine, even if you only have access to a small piece of property. Every step your horse takes makes his hooves and his body healthier, his immune system better. And it really is not that difficult or expensive to figure it out. Much cheaper than barns and stalls.

> **Paddock Paradise: A Guide to Natural Horse Boarding** This book by Jaime Jackson begins with a study of horses in the wild, then describes many plans for getting your horses out 24/7, in replication of the wild. The designs are all very specific, but by reading the entire book you begin to deduce what's really important and what's not so important, and why. We didn't follow any of his plans, but we have one pasture that's probably an acre and a half and two much smaller ones (photos on our website www.thesoulofahorse.com). All of them function very well when combined with random food placement. They keep our horses on the move, as they would be in the wild. The big one is very inexpensively electrically-fenced. *Paddock Paradise* is available, as are all of Jaime's books, at **http://www.paddockparadise.com/**

Also see the video **The Soul of a Horse Paddock Paradise: What We Did, How We Did It, and Why** on The Soul of a Horse Channel on YouTube.

New resources are regularly updated on Kathleen's and my: **www.theSoulofaHorse.com** or our blog **http://thesoulofahorse.com/blog**

Liberated Horsemanship at:
http://www.liberatedhorsemanship.com/
Scroll down to the fifth Article in the column on the
right entitled Barefoot Police Horses

**An article about the Houston Mounted Patrol on our
website:** Houston Patrol Article

The following videos on various subjects, all found on
The Soul of a Horse Channels on YouTube and
Vimeo:

Why Are Our Horses Barefoot?

Why Our Horses Eat from the Ground

Finding The Soul of a Horse

Joe and Cash: Relationship First!

**The Soul of a Horse Paddock Paradise: What We Did,
How We Did It, and Why**

Don't Ask for Patience – God Will Give You a Horse

Video: Shod Hoof
Video: Barefoot Hoof

Find a recommended trimmer in your area:

http://www.aanhcp.net

http://www.americanhoofassociation.org

http://www.pacifichoofcare.org

http://www.liberatedhorsemanship.com/

Valuable Links on Diet and Nutrition:

Dr. Juliette Getty's website:
http://gettyequinenutrition.biz/

Dr. Getty's favorite feed/forage testing facility:
Equi-Analytical Labs:
http://www.equi-analytical.com

For more about pretty much anything in this book please visit one of these websites:

www.thesoulofahorse.com

http://thesoulofahorse.com/blog

The Soul of a Horse Fan Page on Facebook

The Soul of a Horse Channels on Vimeo and YouTube

Joe and The Soul of a Horse on Twitter @Joe_Camp

Made in United States
Orlando, FL
28 December 2022

27831262R10050